A Curse on the Fairest Joys

A Curse on the Fairest Joys

Poems by

Martha K. Grant

for Brenda —
diving deep,
listening well.
Happy
creating !

Martha K Grant

Kelsay Books

Cover Art: *Beltane Fires,* shibori-dyed fiber art by the author
Cover photograph: Susie Monday

ISBN 13: 978-0692426869

Kelsay Books
Aldrich Press
www.kelsaybooks.com

Acknowledgments

"A Heart That Listens" was selected for *Poetry on the Move*, VIA Metropolitan Transit

"To Someone's Daddy at IH-10 & Woodlawn" appeared in the San Antonio *Express-News*

"Standing in the Gap" and "The Artist vs. the Poet" appeared in *Voices de la Luna*

"The Committee" appeared in *Why Good People Do Bad Things*, by James Hollis, PhD

Sections of the poem "How It Came To This" were included under another title in the anthology *Unruly Catholic Women Writers, Vol. II,* SUNY Press

"Self-portrait at a Borrowed Cottage" is titled after a Jane Hirshfield poem

"I Could Only Believe in a God Who Could Dance" is titled after a quote by Friedrich Nietzsche

"Stillborn" was published in *The Enigmatist* and nominated for a Pushcart Prize

Author photo by Melanie Rush Davis

Contents

III

IV

I

Descanso

The Ghost Father

*I found that the story of her death stood in the way of every other thing,
that no other poems could be written until I wrote about this.*
—Kathleen Bonanno, *Slamming Open the Door*

Like smoke wafting from a toxic fire,
he rose up out of the body
and onto the front-page photo,
threading his deadly tentacles
through the headlines.
He gathered his own ammunition
from the report—
didn't drink, didn't own a gun—
then smudged me
with his unholy incense.
The Ghost Father clouded
the memory of my own father
pacing sad and grim-faced
as I was told the news,
and overlaid another scene,
in sharper focus now:
him cleaning his guns,
for hunting season,
a cold beer at his elbow.

The Ghost Father
wrote a new catechism
of possiblity, of lies,
preached a new gospel
of wariness, doubt,
as he seated himself
in my father's place
at the head of the table.

Target Practice

If it's true what they said,
that her father didn't own a gun,
could he have aimed well enough
to hit the target of his daughter's head?

Had he rented a rifle,
driven out to the same field
for days (weeks, months) of practice—
on melons, maybe,
though Texas limestone
was plentiful, and free?

Setting chunk upon chunk
to her four foot height,
did he wear heavy gloves
to move the stones,
wary of snakes, scorpions?

Rock would shatter, but cleanly.
Canteloupe would splatter
like a child's head—
three shots, the paper said—

the sweet flesh, juicy seeds
coming to rest
among the prickly pear,
agarita, mesquite.

The 200 Block of Watchill Drive

He parked at the edge of the woods
a few miles from their house, left two
white envelopes on the front seat.
One for their mother: "I am sorry."
One for the coroner requesting cremation.
He opened the trunk and slung the rifle
over his shoulder, slammed the door
for the last time. He led them deep into the cover
of mesquite, hackberry, live oak. His jeans
tore on the fence he had to climb over,
his children small enough to slip safely through
the opening he made, holding the strands
of barbed wire apart with his bare hands.

Walk With Me

Walk with me, Hecate.
Or rather, sit me down.
Tug at the hem of my skirt,
the fringe of my scarf
as I—yet again—
wander aimlessly past,
scanning the horizon.

Like one pats the couch cushion
inviting the cat to join
in the doing of nothing,
pat the dust
beside where you sit,
O Guardian of the Crossroads,
smooth a place for me,
ease me down.

Descanso

I didn't think of asking to be taken there,
to be shown the field where it happened.
Had I been older than nine,
I might have thought of bringing flowers
to lay at the spot where she died,
clipping roses for her
from mother's garden like we did
for the May processions
where we circled the church
singing to the Virgin,
hymns we'd memorized in Latin,
unaware they were petitions
for Her protection
as we carried our wilting offerings—
thorns removed as instructed—
up the center aisle
to lay at Her feet.

The Memory Game, 1952

Ready with paper and pencils, we sat on the floor
in her den and studied the lumps in the cloth for clues.

When her mother pulled the towel off the tray,
we focused on the display of familiar objects.

Who has the best memory? What will you recall
in the short time you'll be given to look?

I scanned the random selection,
reciting to myself this household litany:

pin cushion—dollar bill—poker chip
spool of thread—pocket knife—pair of dice

When the tray was again covered, I remembered:
pink rosary—cap pistol—Brownie pin

The prize was a holy card with a familiar image:
a guardian angel leading a girl and boy

across a bridge. I was disappointed to win it.
I wanted something to play with.

Requiem

Searching the newspaper archives once again,
I unspool those October headlines and photographs:
two small bodies under white sheets, the body of a man
in t-shirt and jeans, a rifle at his side,
the reporter quoting the coroner:
the girl had been running to protect her little brother,
already dropped with a single shot.
Signs of a scuffle. Three shots to her head,
a final bullet into the father's mouth.

It was a fourth grade Monday morning
when I was told the news, held on my mother's lap
as we scanned the front page; then at school
Sister Matilda selected six of us for pallbearers,
and some of us whispered that one classmate
should not have been chosen,
wasn't *really* Joan's friend like we were.

We wore our Sunday shoes, white carnations
pinned to the starched lapels of our uniforms.
With six khaki-clad first grade boys, friends of Johnny's,
we followed in slow procession up the center aisle
behind their small white coffins. The pipe organ mourned
in the choir loft. The eulogy droned.
In the pallbearers' front pew I tucked my chin
into my collarbone to inhale the comfort
of the flower's scent, like ether, anesthetizing.

On the way to the graveyard we fidgeted
in silence on the slick seats of the shiny limo,
under the stern gaze and pinched faces of our teachers,
the dark sunglasses of the expressionless driver
reflecting in his rearview mirror. I scuffed
my black patent shoes along the fake grass

19

under the dark green cemetery tent
where we startled at her mother's cry,
the sudden sound of heavy machinery
ratcheting down its precious cargo.

Back in the classroom, one desk missing,
the space quietly closing up.

Prom Night

A young man in a rented tuxedo
shuffles to the door
clutching a white box,
a carnation corsage
nestled in tissue visible
through the cellophane window.
When he guides me to the dance floor,
I slide my hand to his shoulder,
burying my face in the ruffle
of white petals ribboned on my wrist.
He holds me shyly,
dancing slowly, and I sigh—
not for him,
but for that single bloom
I was asked to sacrifice
to the lid of the lowered casket.

"THY WILL BE DONE"

You didn't live long enough to discover what pizza was
but I think you'd like that there's a pizza parlor

across the street from where you lie with your father and brother.
You may not like this inscription on the triple headstone, though,

with its chiseled taunting. However well-intentioned,
I am not convinced that Jesus-in-the-garden praying

above your father's head really believes God's will was done.
I look up from the pencil rubbing I've made of your name

on the grey granite and I see us there, years later, laughing
in a back booth at lunch, after sneaking away from school

to this side of town where no one knew us or recognized
our uniforms, no one to rat on us sharing a beer,

contraband cigarettes, and a thick slice of cheese pizza,
our navy skirts hidden beneath the table, not revealing

our Catholic school identity, not earning us a detention,
a suspension, a black mark on our record for life.

A Heart That Listens

—1 Kings 3:9

Give your servant *lebh shomea*,
the prophet prays—
a listening heart—
to hear what ears
might otherwise miss,
like the sound of grace
going about its business,
carefully peeling cobwebs
from the corners of your walls
and weaving them
into lace curtains
to replace
your blackout shades.

Good Dirt

On this fall morning of hunting season,
my father eases himself from my car
leaning heavily on his walking stick,
then straightens to something less
than the six feet he used to be.
How many years since he abandoned
the old cabin and retired his deer rifles
and the wool hunting shirt,
soft as a baby blanket,
that now hangs in my closet?
Hot oatmeal before dawn,
then the crisp chill in the blind,
listening for the snap of twigs under hooves,
only his frosted breath for company.
Ten feet onto this rocky property
where new homesites such as mine
are being carved from former ranch land
is all he can manage now.
He turns an ear toward the sound
of a doe and her fawn moving deeper
into the cedars. I watch him
test the ground with his stick,
poking at it, stirring the soil with the tip.
Good dirt, he says, inscribing
a benediction on my land.
This is good dirt.

Next In Line

My father stands at the foot of his bed
in the middle of the night,
his thin pajamas sagging
on his bony frame.
He clings to the mahogany poster.
Waiting in line, he says to the dark.
My mother pats his pillow, urges him back.
No, I'll lose my place.
He shuffles to the post
at the other corner of the bed,
says he's making progress,
says he has to *see the manager over there.*
He points toward the old bookcase
where his parents and his grandmother
wait on the top shelf
in small ornate frames,
watching him through sepia eyes,
calling his name.

To Someone's Daddy at IH-10 & Woodlawn

Who was it you were talking to,
your shaggy grey head bobbing
as I inched down the exit ramp?
Did you have daughters?
Did they know where you were?

The railing where you sat, daily,
under the interstate overpass
is empty now since you died.
I wanted to love you, old man,
I might have loved you,
but the light at the Woodlawn intersection
was never long enough to let me.
I forgot you as soon as I passed,
you and your cockeyed baseball cap,
your baggy navy pants,
that stained plaid shirt
buttoned clumsily,
one unused buttonhole left over
at the end of your shirttail.

II

Standing in the Gap

The Artist vs. the Poet

My two muses are jealous stepsisters,
escapees from an obscure fairy tale,
vying for the starring role in my creative life.
When one is in residence, having bolted
the lock behind her on entering,
she commands my rapt attention
to her flirtation or outright seduction.
But the other pouts on the studio porch,
pacing and chain smoking,
rattling the door handle,
making faces in the windows.

Some days they stand at a collaborative impasse,
shoulder to shoulder in the door frame
blocking the light,
sturdy arms folded across stubborn chests,
the paint-spattered artist smock
and the ink-stained poet shirt
hanging limp and lifeless
on a single peg.

Just Two?

You are sitting in a wagon being drawn by a horse whose reins you hold.
There are two inside of you who can steer.
—Kabir

This wagon is full to overflowing,
like a kindergarten class
on a field trip to the country,
where the farmer has come to regret
his idea of a hayride,
and how his offering of the reins
to the small hands nearest him
prompted the tumbling
of bodies from the back of the wagon
to the front, clamoring
for a chance to drive.
Me! My turn! I was next!

Though some proved to be instinctively better
at the task than others,
some tight little fists
have yet to be pried loose.

The Committee

The rude one is the first of many
who populate my inner committee,
an unruly group of stubborn complexes
who try to run my life.
My vigilant effort to tame these insubordinates
is ongoing, endless. I've wheedled and flattered
and, when that didn't work, actually reasoned
with the most recalcitrant;
it only makes them more determined.

Besides, they have my number.
They've sat too often with my therapist,
wringing their collective hands,
clucking sympathetically,
when all along they were
gathering ammunition.

Now they are doling out assignments—
I can hear the papers shuffling—
and what's more,
they are calling in new recruits
from the streets.

If You Are Lucky

The buried wealth is your pay for doing the demolition,
the pick and shovel work
—Rumi, "The Pick Axe"

On the other hand, put your ear to the floorboards
before prying them up—you might hear

your unconfessed sins gathering for a poker game
in the basement, having dusted off the table

and rearranged the chairs to accommodate the crowd;
how they now ante up all those old transgressions,

the stakes higher and higher with each round.
You'll know by the raucous, raunchy laughter

who has folded and who's still in the game.

In Line for the Sweat Lodge, Eavesdropping

Someone says last night I heard coyotes singing,
   says every morning I watch my desert wake up,
      says there might be leprechauns around here.

Someone says Freud's a cultural product,
   says the meaning is in the juxtaposition,
      says any fool knows that.

Someone says baseball is about the whole game of life,
   says I can't go back to Philly kissing birds,
      says I gotta ship five loads of cattle out of Angelo.

Someone says you know you can buy black powder cartridges,
   says nobody bites me and lives to tell about it,
      says you don't have to have water to motorboat.

Someone says she talks to her brain all the time,
   says pay attention, numbskull,
      says apotheosis.

Ceremony

We circle the fire pit for the sweat lodge
where large rocks pop and crackle in the flames,
exploding an offering of sparks, our prayers
ferried up into the night sky.

Like pilgrims at a foreign temple we wait
to give ourselves over to this ancient sacred ritual,
clutching towels to wrap around our nakedness,
our ambivalence.

When the shaman's drum invites us in,
we shed them at the entrance, crawl
on hands and knees through the tent flap.

Hip to hip in the close and holy dark,
we beg for mercy as the hot rocks
are shoveled in. Some of them will split open.

Standing in the Gap

It is not clear to me
whether the view from my window
is up, into the infinite expanse
of the night sky—or down,
through the grid
of a glass-bottomed boat,
into equally mysterious depths
of a raging sea.
I stand in the gap.

This is not the first time
I have not known
down from up.
This is not the first time
Light has shone
in an uncomprehending
darkness.

III

How It Came To This

Stones in Your Soul Shoes

Still limping along with
stones in your soul shoes,
stopping at times
to steady against a tree,
a mailbox,
strip off a sock, shake it out,
expecting a pebble to skitter
on the pavement
where you can inspect it,
turn it over in your hand
and face a choice—

to fling it off the path,
or drop it back
into its familiar nest
in your shoe.

Small Talk

That spring of third grade, we sold Girl Scout cookies
at my father's office, 50¢ a box, Joan and I going from

desk to desk as his coworkers teased us, wanting all vanilla
or all chocolate instead of half of each,

the way they were packaged, while my mother leaned
on his secretary's desk, making small talk.

Later we romped in the spray of the sprinkler in my yard,
our striped Brownie t-shirts soaked, our wet bangs dripping

into our eyes, the sodden fresh-cut grass staining our bare feet.
The neighbor's black dachshund slept in the sun, basking

on a white square stepping stone in the garden, Joan giggling
that the dog reminded her of a burnt wiener on a slice of bread.

She did not live long enough to grow up to be a poet.

Album

See, she's the one in the ruffled dress
at my birthday party. And here
we're doing the Hokey Pokey
at the Brownie picnic. This one
is our First Communion photo—
we're on the top row of the bleachers
in identical veils with a sprig of fake
lily of the valley, our hands posed
around new prayer books
and tangled rosaries.

In the middle of this sea of smiling children—
boys in white suits on the right,
girls in white lace on the left—
a contrast in his black cassock,
that's the pastor, who'd preside
at her funeral a few years later.
He's smiling too.

Oh, the rip in the photo,
down through his grinning face?
A recent tear, my own father's doing,
once he learned the truth of my childhood—
one father avenging another Father's evil.

How It Came To This

As the caterpillar chooses the fairest leaves to lay her eggs on,
so the priest lays his curse on the fairest joys.
—William Blake, *Proverbs of Hell*

i.

That first day of first grade, that small nun
with the starched linen tight around her stern face,
her black serge habit girded with a red cord dangling
a wooden rosary, an ominous crucifix;
that scarlet embroidery bleeding a crown of thorns
on her breast; that foreboding that gnawed
an enlarging space between a young girl
and her mother's retreating back;
the feel of the nun's hands clenched
on small trembling shoulders;
the sound of the sentencing:
I will hold her, mother, and you go.

ii.

The new rosary is snug in its box, the glass beads
resting in a nest of cotton she'll save for later,
for scrubbing pink polish from chewed nails.
She's been told it has no spiritual value yet,
unblessed—just a strand of metal links,
fake crystal and a Jesus fastened
to his silver-plated cross.
She'll take it to the priest.
He gathers the beads into his left palm,
placing the cross on top, Jesus face up.
She waits in practiced reverence,
counting the decades of precise black buttons,
perfectly spaced, trailing like the Sorrowful Mysteries,

neck to hem, down the front of his long cassock.
She holds her breath, watching his flattened right hand,
cuticles and nails gnawed, transcribe its own cross
above her pale pink, future prayers.

iii.

At the rectory door, reporting as instructed, she waits
on the wooden porch, shifting from one small saddle oxford
to the other, the harsh buzzer jarring. She presses it just once—
quickly—wanting no one to answer.
Not wanting. Wanting.

iv.

The red floral pattern in the drapes, the slant of school day sun
through the tilted blinds that stripe his office wallpaper,
the scratchy texture of green desk blotter on bare bottom.
You will learn to like it,
his low voice echoing still.

v.

She leaves her lunch bag under the bus stop bench,
hoping no one notices, wipes her sticky hands
on the pleats of her uniform skirt,
this parcel of memory, the torn panties,
the soggy tissues wadded in the wrinkled sack,
disposed of now, shoved toward the back,
in the shadow of a bag lady slumped
on the green-slatted seat, clutching

her own dirty possessions,
each of them wondering
how it came to this.

vi.

She lines up with her class along the side aisle of church
and leans her cheek against the cool stone wall,
rehearsing from the checklist of sins the nun has read,
her failings responsible for the savage drama played out
on the walls overhead,
the Stations of the Cross looming, indicting.
Jesus Scourged, Nailed, Crucified.

Her small voice trembles, her palms clammy—
it's him behind this veiled window now,
breathing, listening—
it's always him,
it will be him for every confession until
she marries and moves from his parish.
Go and sin no more,
his ritual script always reads.
Yes, Father. Thank you, Father,
her programmed reply.

vii.

Her mother looks up from the sewing table, the bolts of red,
purple, green brocades, the satin linings, the gold braid—
soon to be new vestments for the family's pastor—
to answer her young teenager's curiosity:
I would think your sense of modesty. . . she offers,

her words trailing off. A proper woman's
abbreviated version of Sex Ed, as though,
modesty above all, no more need be said.

viii.

Making rounds, he visits after a teenage surgery.
Unaccustomed to being a patient and self-conscious
in a hospital gown, she does not know what to say,
what social niceties are expected of her.
Accustomed to being a priest, he suggests:
Would you like my blessing?
She feels remiss, chastised—
she should have thought to ask—
didn't she know better?
Yes, Father. Thank you, Father.

ix.

She knows her once-bright lipstick is a telltale smear,
but there's no other entry than this front door.
She smooths her skirt, tries to straighten the taffeta lining,
the recently wrinkled petticoats. With deep inhale of bravado,
she manages a casual face, enters through laughter and liquor
in her living room, sashays past the poker table and greets
her parents' friends. He squints at her from behind his fat cigar,
his longneck beer, his stacks of red and blue chips.
He knows he will hear yet another of her confessions
next Saturday when she is required to report what happened
in the back seat of the car this evening.

x.

The thirteenth photo in the wedding album,
or rather, the empty plastic sleeve where it would be,
should she choose to include it,
that photo of the smiling groom, the wistful bride
kneeling before the altar,
the priest with his thick gilt-edged
prayer book looming over them,
handing over his one-time prey
to her unsuspecting prince.

xi.

What would you have done if you had known?
she asks her father when the old memories
begin to break open, surfacing from the deep,
decades after the fact.
I suppose I would've had to shoot 'im,
he says without hesitation, his response
a retroactive safety net rolled out under her childhood,
stretched taut to catch her free-fall into the terror
of long-buried truth.
After her mother's assessments—
You must have fallen through the cracks, and
Your father and I decided there is no room for hate—
he says she doesn't speak for him,
but the latest edition of the Catholic catechism
soon appears on the coffee table,
in lieu of the usual candies, magazines.

Where Are Their Mothers?

I sit in my mother's wheelchair beside her bed,
my feet on the bedrail, watching
the rise and fall of her chest, and I catch
my own breath with each twelve-second pause of hers,
and exhale with her every rasping inhale.
Her glazed eyes question the closet door,
the bedpost, the corner of the ceiling.
One gnarled hand struggles free
of the quilted satin covers and gestures
with a bony, bird-like claw toward visions
only she can see. She asks of the air:
The children. There are so many children.
Where are their mothers?
I coax her hand back into its nest
under the blanket,
straighten the silky peach comforter
she inherited from her mother—
her namesake and mine—
whom she sometimes imagines
sits on a chair at the foot of the bed,
her back to both of us.

Estate Sale

May I have her piano? Are the vintage perfume bottles valuable?
I've always loved this photograph. Save the clock on the mantel for me.

Whispers drift through the rooms of my grandparents' house
as I linger at the dressing table in my mother's girlhood bedroom

where I used to sit as a child and preen in her mirror, peeking
behind the flowered chintz skirt into the dark shelf where

blue and amber vials of cologne still hold traces of a scent.
Serenade. Tabu. My Sin.

Was it *Scandal* she was wearing the night she waited and waited,
listening for an echo of footsteps on the wooden porch?

Perching first on the couch, then the arm of the chair,
the piano stool, she tried not to wrinkle the gown she wears

in this faded photo still on the dresser, the pink satin and chiffon
she designed for just that evening. She was certain she caught

the glint of setting sun on a shiny fender as his '36 roadster
rounded the corner. She checked the clock on the mantel,

her lipstick in the mirror, while the fragrance
on her wrist, her small cleavage, behind her ears—

those pulse points recommended by the beauty magazines—
faded, and a young man circled the block, again and again,
before heading for home.

Waiting for the Medical Examiner, 7 a.m.

I soothe my fingertips across her cooling brow,
down her smooth, now sunken, cheeks,
slide strands of her hair through my fingers,
much of it grey, enough of it still
streaked with the brown of her youth,
hair an ambivalent color, undecided,
as if unwilling to commit to, admit to
old age, her hair outwaiting
the rest of her body,
and winning.

I play the fine strands
over and over, like strings
of an ancient instrument
humming at my touch,
or like a finger circling
the wet lip of a wine glass,
trying to make it
sing to me.

Amazing Grace

Zippered into a body bag
the color of burgundy wine,
a color she would have been
pleased to wear any other day,
she's rolled out her front door
by portly gentlemen in somber grey suits.
Barefoot on the damp pebbled sidewalk,
I follow the gurney to the curb,
crooning softly to myself:
Amazing grace, how sweet the sound,
my sister's hand in mine,
our brother behind us,
the sibling fond of proclaiming
that our clan can't sing,
we aren't a musical family.
It is morning, early,
and still I dare to sing,
louder now, daring to alter the lyrics,
declaring my mother not a wretch,
but a soul, a soul like me.

Pilgrimage to a Different God

Having scrambled down
from the pedestals
we'd put them on,
our gods now stand aside,
fall in behind us,
closing ranks.

Their footfalls throb
a drumbeat, urging
us on, erasing
the path back
to our old lives.

Now and then
one of us stops
to shake
a crippling stone
from a shoe.

Silence Happens, Sometimes

The profound well of silence at the heart of our being will not fail us.
—Thomas Merton

It may lumber in slowly,
like an aging grandfather
shuffling toward his rocker after dinner,
waving off the offer of your arm,
refusing to be hurried.
Sometimes you invite it
with the steady thump of a drum,
which, when it ceases, leaves
a subtle vibration you fall into,
expectant and sighing.

Sometimes it happens unexpectedly,
dropping a stone into a bottomless well
as you lean over the damp, lichened edge,
squinting down the dark,
hardly daring to breathe or blink,
not wanting to miss the *plink*
that never comes.

Scattering the Dead Skins

Scattering the dead skins
of an old self behind her,
she's wandering deeper
into the forest, but
unlike Gretel,
with no breadcrumbs
and no intention of
turning back and reclaiming
those old lives that lie,
discarded, on the dark path.

I pray the birds from that old story
will migrate into hers,
erasing the trail,
forcing her onward,
as she goes to meet
whatever witch awaits.

IV

Strange Angels

FoxSpeak, July 22

We cannot know the language of foxes.
When one of these native speakers entered the yard,
settled on her haunches and turned to stare at me
reading on the porch, my finger marked the place in my book
and my breath caught and held like it did when we were kids
playing dead, discovering how much subtle movement
breathing demands of the body,
hoping the designated adversary would not notice,
would take us for dead and move on.

When the fox uttered an emphatic *roff!* what was I to do then?
Marking the moment on the calendar was but a meager effort
to honor the message, hardly adequate to decipher it.

If I tell you this visitation was on the feast day of Mary Magdalene
whose gnostic gospel describes how the Teacher spoke to *her*,
you might understand why this missed opportunity
haunts me each July anniversary.

Was it that I could not know the fox's meaning?
Or that the process repeated twice more?
She would rise, slink twenty feet closer,
her tail horizontal like a rudder,
and facing me, she would sit again
and speak again her monosyllabic gospel—
and now, how not to think of a certain cock
crowing, thrice?

When a sacred emissary dares to turn and face you,
would you not also back away?

Stillborn

Thinner than matchsticks,
the tiny fingers curl
in a pink question mark
frozen in time.
By way of answer,
I ease my own finger into
his birdlike grasp—
as though he expected this
all along, this one
exquisite moment
what he'd remember
for the eternity into which
he was prematurely thrust.

Surprised at the soft flexibility
of his fingers, I stroke
the underside of them,
the half inch from palm
to fingertips, over and over,
as if beckoning,
watching his fingers spring back
into that questioning curve,
beckoning.

On the Down Escalator to Baggage Claim

The pink bundle whimpering
on her mother's shoulder has set off
a chain reaction in my body.
With the mewing of her newborn,
all my systems go on alert, that longing
for an infant to snuggle
in the hollow of the sternum,
for the sweet scent of that damp crease
in a baby's neck,
a reawakening after thirty years,
my breasts tingling with the body memory
of milk letting down, triggered
by the cry of a hungry baby.

If I offer this weary young woman
a credit card for the temporary exchange
of her tiny, now howling, daughter,
would she trust my help
while she claims her luggage?
I would not worry should the mother—
and my card—
disappear into the crowd.

What Is the Knocking?

A golden-fronted woodpecker
raps on the eaves above the door,
forsaking the acres of oaks
just beyond, searching instead
for whatever sustenance
might lie dormant in the cedar beams.
It is early morning, the sixth
of January, the Epiphany,
and I wonder if my caller
might be one of the Magi,
clutching that gold to his chest,
lost on the way to Bethlehem,
a couple thousand years late,
many thousand miles off track,
having misread the light
of a certain star.

Three Strange Angels

It's somebody wants to do us harm.
No, no, it is the three strange angels.
Admit them, admit them.
—D. H. Lawrence

Hang their ragged wraps
on the rack in the hall,
line up their battered boots on the mat.
Show them to the table you have set
with your best china and silver,
your delicate crystal goblets.
You will not need place cards;
they will know where to sit.
See your guests' faces soften
in the glow of candlelight,
flush with your wine.

Spread pallets on the floor for
the ones who would stay the night.
Do not be tempted to sleep
with one eye open,
one ear cocked for the sound
of dark wings unfurling,
clinking against the chandelier,
sweeping your fragile heirlooms
from the mantel, knocking askew
the family portraits that line
the hall. In the morning,
you will sweep the shattered glass
from the hearth.

Self-Portrait at a Borrowed Cottage

Sphinx-like on my lap,
her paws in a studied pose
and squinting slanty-eyed
like she's proud of herself,
the resident B&B feline
is on assignment.
She dreams of Egypt, the Nile,
her cat goddess ancestors
and the minions she is ordained
to protect, of which I am one,
pinioned as I am
under the weight of her mythology.
My idle fingertips make tracks
on her sleek back,
raking over and over,
an offering to the ancient ones
who look with favor on
our shared stony silence.

Arachne at the Mailbox at Equinox

Straddling the seasons,
Grandmother Spider
weaves her alphabet of silk
in a scaffold of spokes stretched
from the top of my mailbox
to the ground. This sentinel
at the curb, deterred by neither
rain nor heat nor gloom of night,
sits at her latticed window,
or tiptoes like a ballerina
on needle-thin legs,
spinning her prey
round and round
in silken shrouds.

I Could Only Believe in a God Who Could Dance

I called him Reebok Jesus back then—
you can tell how long ago by the footwear,
and the fact that I was still praying to him.
Or rather, trying to find a way to.
Nothing else was working so I began to envision him
as the 33-year old he was before he died,
but in modern dress. I allowed him his brown hair
and that beard, but neatly trimmed.
Like playing paper dolls, I outfitted him in
tight jeans and a James Dean t-shirt, white,
the sleeves rolled up, a pack of cigarettes tucked.
And those Reeboks. White.
I never determined whether he smoked,
but it wouldn't have killed him if he had.

I would close my eyes and move to the music
on the stereo, imagine him just in front of me,
mirroring my movements.
He eventually disappeared into the ether,
replaced by other iconography of the Sacred,
in feminine form. Sophia, Tara, Kwan Yin.

Recently he showed up in a dream,
older, grayer, looking for all the world
like a modern Muslim cleric.
Said his Mother told him about me.

Who Else Matters?

God and I have become like two fat people living in a tiny boat.
We keep bumping into each other and laughing.
—Hafiz

Resting the dripping oars across her wide lap
and eyeing the lavish expanse we lazily drift on,
she says, *Take off your clothes, let's go for a swim.*

We hadn't spoken for hours. Startled, I argue,
That's like a mother telling her child,
'I'm cold, put a sweater on.'
You're the one who wants to swim.

Good point, she admits;
now, take off your clothes.

But everyone will see me naked!
I'm whining now, clutching my jacket
to my chest. She's impatient.
You're not wearing a nametag.
Who will know it's you?

I'd stomp my feet, but that would rock
this tiny boat, dumping us both
into the deep.
Now I'm pleading:

Who else matters, besides you?

To Kwan Yin, Goddess of Compassion

You've seen me with hands on hips,
stomping my feet. You've caught
the vibrations of this restless mind,
incessant assessments, petulant
discourse, peevish complaints.

I've seen you rolling your eyes,
tsk-tsk-ing as you follow behind me,
surveying the damage,
setting things aright in my wake.
Stop now. Stop me now.
Put your hands on these shoulders,
turn me to know your gaze,
your warm breath on my face.
Teach me your way of compassion.
Begin with me.

Trusting the Long Holy Silence

Midwifing that pause in conversation
where we find the quiet awkward

and, unable to bear it,
finally mention the weather,

while waiting instead,
breath after breath,

might have opened a space
we could hold between us

for the hush rushing in
after the rain.

Comes the Day

The wayfarer bends
in unwitting genuflection
to retie a shoe, notices
small flowers pushing up
between the rough stones,
peeking through cracks
in the hard road,
their fresh faces stretching
toward the light.

Your Prayer Rug

It doesn't matter which direction you point your prayer rug.
—Rumi

It matters that you take it down from the shelf,
unroll it, shake it out and spread it.
Anywhere will do.

If its tangled fringe bothers you, stoop to comb it
with your fingers, then surrender. Lower your body
whatever degree it agrees to. Then surrender more.

It doesn't matter what direction your head is pointed.
Maybe it's your left side the gods need facing them.
Your big toes, your right ear.

Let your heartbeat add its cadence to the earth's vibration.
Feel your breath feed the earth as your body will one day.
Maybe soon.

Feel the sun, wind, the rain on your back
tender what brought you here, your tattered rug, its fringe.
Feel the quiet untangling of the knots.

About the Author

*Let the beauty we love be what we do; there are a hundred ways
to kneel and kiss the ground.*
—Rumi

Martha K. Grant's various muses jostle each other for a starring role in her creative life. She hopes to negotiate a collaboration between them, layering her poetry into her painting, calligraphy, collage and fiber art. A sixth generation Texan, she lives with her husband and a temperamental cat in the Hill Country northwest of San Antonio, sharing the property with deer, porcupines, skunks, roadrunners and a hundred other species of birds.